Mining

Written by Jane Drake with Ann Love
Illustrated by Pat Cupples

Kids Can Press

"Your coach says we've raised enough money to go to the Junior Miners' Hockey Tournament out east," Dad tells the twins. "You'll play teams from all over the country."

"Wow! Can I get new ice skates?" Jamie asks, unpacking his equipment bag.

"Your skates still fit," Mom says. "Besides, skates don't grow on trees. Think of all the things that go into making them. Leather, plastic, steel …"

"Steel just comes from a factory, doesn't it?" asks Trish.

"Actually, it all starts with minerals and metals found in rock in the ground," Mom explains. "Like the molybdenum from the mine where I work."

"No way," says Jamie.

"Why don't you come and see for yourself?" suggests Mom.

"Then I'll take you to the steel mill where molybdenum and other metals are added to liquid iron to make the steel tough enough for skate blades," offers Dad.

"Cool!" the twins shout together.

3

Driving to the mine, Mom explains that it takes a lot of people, money and time to develop a mine. Mining companies use special equipment — even satellites — to look for clues above and below the earth's surface that help them detect valuable minerals hidden underground. If they find a large deposit, and get government permission, they may start a mine.

aerial survey plane

magnetometer

core drill

"Those workers over there are geologists," Mom says. "They are drilling holes that go down farther than many skyscrapers go up. If they're lucky, the rock samples they bring to the surface will show signs of gold and minerals containing molybdenum or iron."

"How did the minerals get there?" asks Trish.

"By chance," Mom explains. "As Earth formed and changed over millions of years, different minerals were trapped in rocks."

rock samples

5

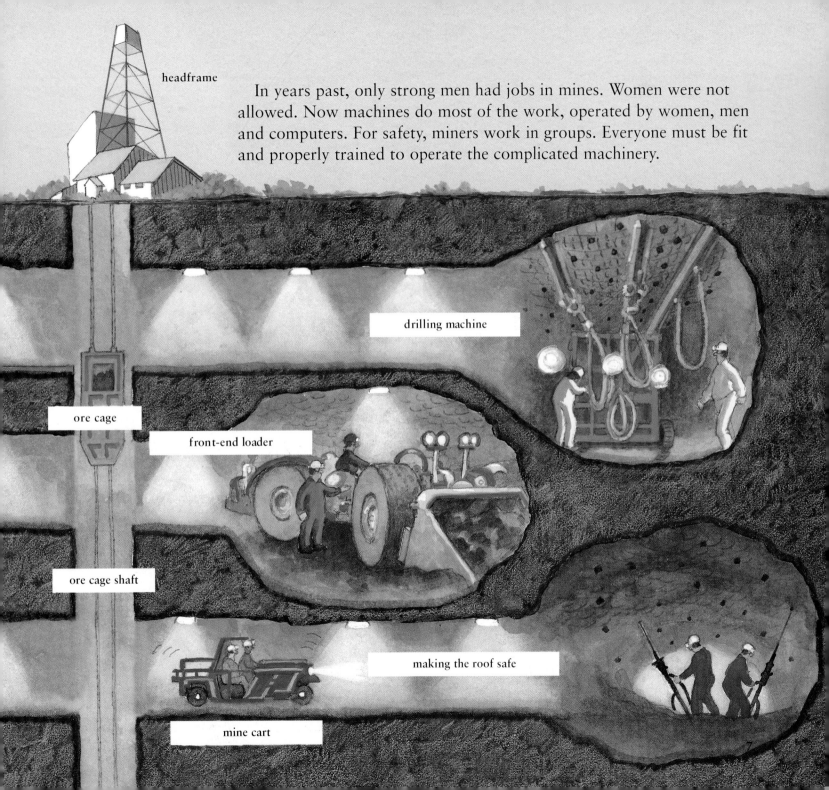

headframe

In years past, only strong men had jobs in mines. Women were not allowed. Now machines do most of the work, operated by women, men and computers. For safety, miners work in groups. Everyone must be fit and properly trained to operate the complicated machinery.

drilling machine

ore cage

front-end loader

ore cage shaft

making the roof safe

mine cart

Mine walls are different colors and textures because rocks usually contain more than one mineral. The mix of minerals and rock is called ore. Ore containing metals often glitters and sparkles. Molybdenum (say "muh-**lib**-duh-numb") ore is silver, white and gray in color.

Where there is a rich vein of ore, workers use drilling machines to drill holes in the mine walls.

ore

drilling machine

8

Blasting experts fill the holes with explosives. When the mine is cleared of people, the team sets off a blast by remote control. Afterward, heavy-duty vehicles haul the ore to an underground crushing station. The crushed ore is then transported to the surface.

"How does it get there?" Jamie yells over the noise of the machinery.

"In a special elevator called an ore cage," shouts Mom.

explosives

On the surface, an enormous crusher smashes the ore into smaller pieces. This makes it easier to separate the valuable metal from the worthless rock called gangue. Conveyor belts or small trains deliver the crushed ore to a nearby concentrating mill.

crusher

At this concentrating mill, machines grind molybdenum ore to a fine powder. In big tubs called flotation cells, the powder is combined with pine oil to make a gritty pulp. Air is forced through the mixture, trapping bits of molybdenum in bubbles floating on the surface. The gangue falls to the bottom.

"At a smelter, the bits of molybdenum ore are heated and refined to form a powder of pure molybdenum," Mom tells them. "This powder is canned and transported by truck to a steel mill, like the one where Dad works."

grinding machine

Hey! This looks like metal. Is it steel yet?

No. Those are iron pellets, the main ingredient in steel. Metals such as molybdenum, copper or nickel are melted with iron to make special types of steel that are shiny, hard and stainless. That means no rust.

At the steel mill, iron ore pellets or scrap iron are put in a huge blast furnace with limestone. The furnace is heated with a fuel called coke — specially treated coal — or electricity. When the furnace is extremely hot, the iron ore and limestone melt. The liquid iron sinks to the bottom of the furnace. The liquid limestone floats to the top and traps bits of impure iron. This waste, called tailings, is collected for disposal.

pouring liquid iron

making ingots

Molybdenum is added to the liquid iron to make stainless steel. This liquid steel can be ladled into molds called ingots. The ingots are heated again and made into sheets, plates, beams and bars. As technology improves, some steel mills are skipping the ingot stage and making slabs of steel with a process called continuous slab casting.

"Regular steel is shipped to factories to make such goods as cars and refrigerators. Stainless steel is made into products such as kitchen sinks and cutlery," Dad tells them. "And skate blades of course," he adds.

making a sheet of steel

rolled sheets of stainless steel

On the way to the tournament, the twins take turns at the airplane window, peppering their parents with questions. They've flown for hours over mountains, forests, fields and cities.

"Are there any mines down there?" Jamie asks.

14

"There are many kinds of mines all across the United States," Mom explains. "Some are underground while others are on the surface. Oil wells are drilled on land and in water, too. Before you play hockey, we'll see a surface coal mine and an oil drilling site. To make your hockey equipment, we need both coal and oil."

Unique machines are used in surface coal mining. Specially trained operators work with computers to make sure this dragline excavator runs smoothly. A gigantic scoop digs out vegetation, topsoil and rock — called the overburden — exposing the coal underneath. The overburden will be dumped back into the mine pit after the coal has been removed so that the area can be reclaimed in the future.

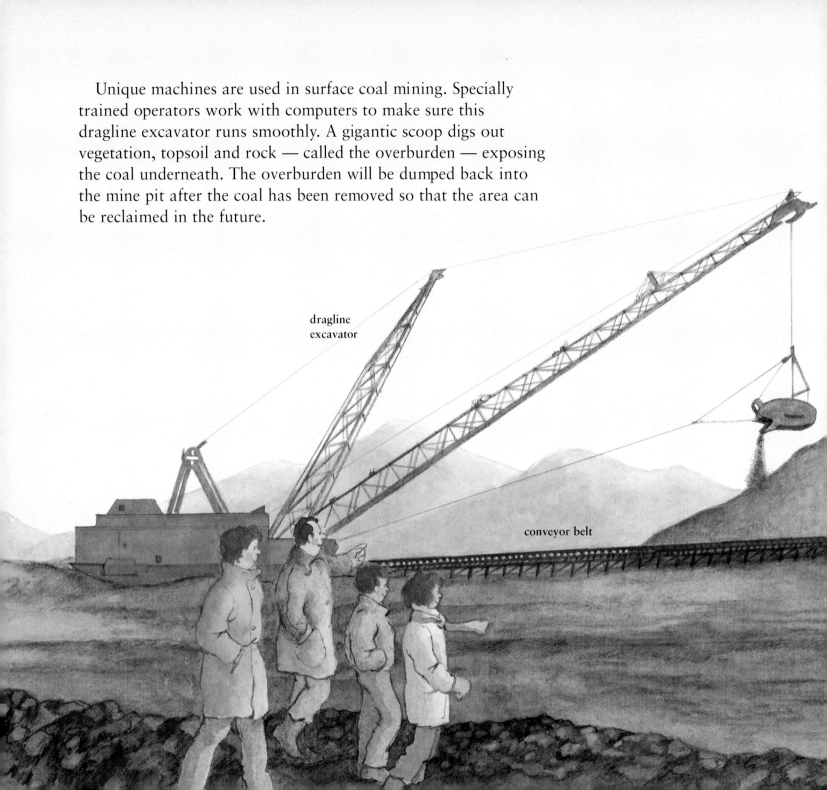

dragline excavator

conveyor belt

Front-end loaders or power shovels load coal into dump trucks that take it to a preparation plant for cleaning, sorting and grading.

"How does coal help us play hockey? It looks like something we grill with," observes Jamie.

"Coal is a burnable fossil fuel," laughs Dad. "But it's mostly used to generate electricity.

"What's a fossil fuel?" asks Trish.

Front-end loader

17

Driving north, Dad explains that fossil fuel deposits were created long ago, some even before dinosaur times. Coal was made when dead plants fell to the bottom of freshwater swamps and the plants were squashed under layers of mud, or sediment. Oil and gas formed below ocean floors when dead plants and tiny animals were sealed in airless pockets under deposits of shale.

Before energy companies explore for oil, they must get drilling rights and permits from landowners and governments. Then geologists look for trapped oil and gas using small explosive charges, listening and recording devices, and computers. When they think they've found oil, companies decide whether or not to drill. Even with all this specialized equipment, only one well in ten makes money. Dry wells are called dusters.

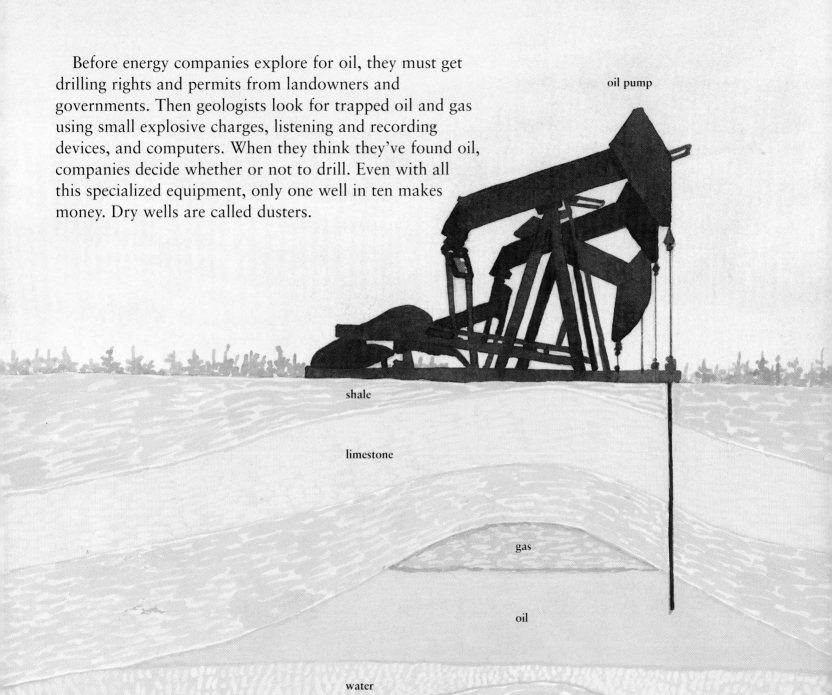

oil pump

shale

limestone

gas

oil

water

This drilling rig is ready to "make hole." The surrounding soil and groundwater has been protected by a cement sleeve. Deep at the bottom of a long pipe, a rotary steel drill studded with industrial diamonds grinds through the rock. Workers called roughnecks operate the drill day and night until the well is finished. A mixture called mud — water, minerals and chemicals — keeps the drill bit slippery so it doesn't get stuck. As the drill goes deeper, more sections of pipe are added on.

Gas is often found along with the oil. A strong valve called a blowout preventer controls the gas pressure underground. When drilling is finished, gas is tapped off at the wellhead, and oil, called crude, is pumped from the ground.

wellhead

drill bit

Crude is trucked from the wellhead to the refinery and stored in large tanks. Pipelines connect the tanks with the oil refinery. Most pipes are buried about six feet underground, where the temperature is steady. In some places, pipes above the ground are warmed in winter so the oil will flow. Pumping stations along the pipeline keep the oil moving. Computers control the flow of oil and check for leaks.

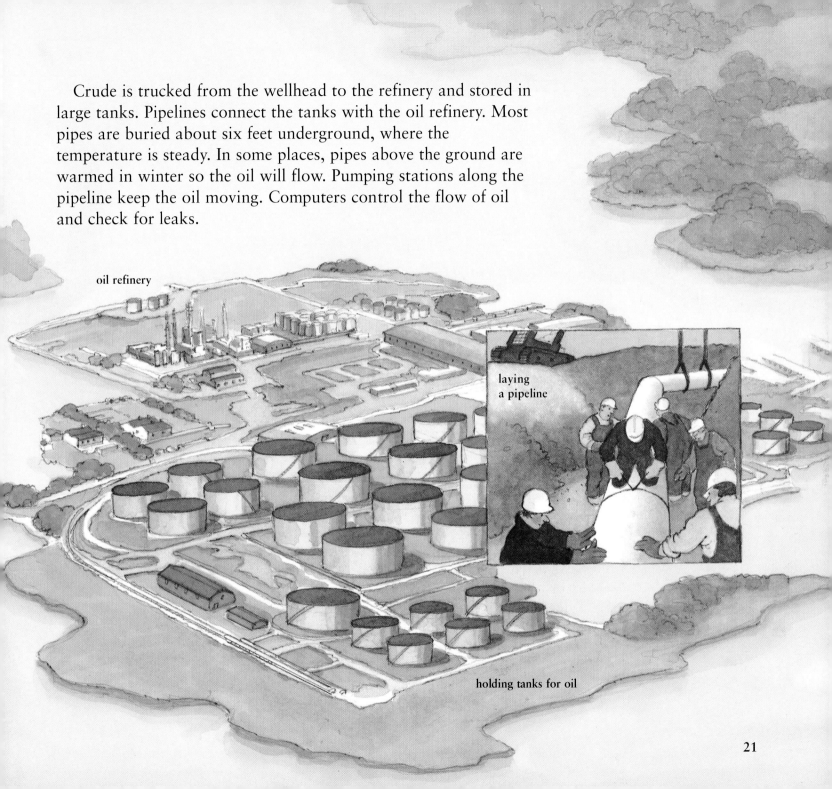

oil refinery

laying a pipeline

holding tanks for oil

At the refinery, crude oil is processed in an enormous distiller called a fractionating tower. Here the crude separates into its various fractions, or parts. When the oil is boiled, it turns to vapor. Each fraction vaporizes at a different temperature. When the vapor is cooled and condensed, the result is gasoline for cars, diesel fuel for trucks or tractors, and heating oil for homes.

tanker truck

Tanks, trucks, rail tankers, ocean tankers and more pipelines carry these oil products across the country and around the world. Oil-refinery leftovers are turned into grease for lubricating machinery and asphalt for paving roads.

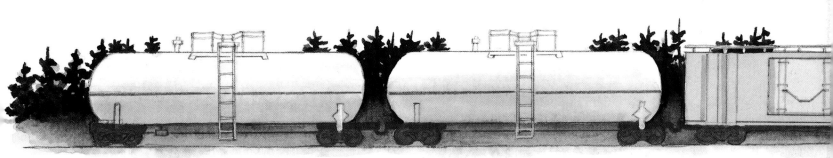

rail tanker

ocean tanker

Most refined oil is burned as fuel to create energy. Energy makes it possible to heat buildings, freeze ice, light streets and power engines. But that's not all oil is used for. Many things that don't look like oil are actually made from oil. Petrochemical plants combine oil by-products with chemicals to make paint, animal feed, medicine, glue, explosives, detergents and plastics. Plastic is used to make thousands of products — from carpets to goalie masks. Using oil by-products saves money and reduces waste.

petrochemical refinery

For Trish and Jamie, mining provides jobs for their parents and makes their favorite game possible. But there's no stickhandling around the fact that mining causes pollution.

Mining always changes the environment. When minerals and oil are removed from the ground, plant life and wildlife are either disturbed or destroyed. And the minerals and oil can never be replaced. They don't regrow the way trees do.

NO DUMPING

26

Refining and milling cause air and water pollution. The furnaces and machines use a lot of energy and create toxic smoke that harms the atmosphere. The enormous quantities of fresh water that are mixed with ore and coal become unsafe for people and wildlife. And accidents, such as oil spills, endanger habitats and wildlife.

People cause all these problems, but they can also control them.

oil-spill cleanup

27

"I can't believe this park was once a coal pit," says Jamie.

"Mining can disturb large areas that must be turned back into habitat for people and wildlife," Dad observes. "Now, mine pits are being filled with overburden and topsoil, and planted with specially developed plants."

"Remember the gangue at the molybdenum mine and the tailings at the steel mill? What about all the waste?" Jamie asks.

"Tailings and gangue are mixed with cement and used to backfill mine tunnels after the ore has been removed," Dad explains. "Mining waste used to be dumped in ugly, lifeless piles. It took years of research to find plants that would grow in these places. Now old mining sites are being turned into places where plants grow and wildlife can live."

People want governments to get tough with companies that pollute. But every person needs to help, by using mining products and fossil fuels with care. Think about the lights you use and the car rides you take. Learn to live by the four R's: reduce, reuse, recycle and refuse.

recreation area on a reclaimed mine site

As the Zamboni prepares the ice for the first game of the tournament, Trish and Jamie look around the arena.

"I can see twenty-three things made from steel or oil," Jamie says.

"Did you count the ref's whistle? That makes twenty-four!" says Trish, pulling on her goalie mask. "Come on, let's play."

1. ceiling girders and beams
2. heating pipes
3. metal benches
4. Zamboni
5. fire alarm
6. metal roll-up door
7. metal face guards on helmets
8. exit sign
9. loudspeaker
10. net frame
11. metal guards on lights
12. clock and scoreboard
13. metal heaters above stands
14. skate guards
15. puck
16. plastic helmet
17. Plexiglas around rink
18. ice (cooled using energy)
19. hockey tape
20. plastic netting
21. garbage can
22. water bottles
23. plastic protectors — shin, shoulder, elbow pads
24. ref's whistle

30

Index

aerial survey plane, 4

blasting experts, 9

chemicals, 20, 24
coal, 12, 15–19, 27, 28
coke, 12
computers, 7, 16, 19, 21
concentrating mills, 10, 11
conveyor belts, 10
core drill, 5
crude, 20, 21, 22
crushers, 6, 10
crushing stations, 9

dragline excavators, 16
drill bit, 20
drilling, 5, 7, 8, 15–16, 19, 20
duster, 19

electricity, 12, 17
elevators, 6, 9. *See also*
    ore cages
energy, 19, 24, 27
environmental concerns, 26–29
explosives, 9, 19, 25

flotation cells, 11
fractionating, 22
fuel, 12, 18–19, 22, 24, 29
furnaces, 12, 27

gangue, 10, 11, 28, 29
gas, 18, 19, 20, 22
geologists, 5, 19

headframes, 6

ingots, 13,
iron, 3, 5, 11, 12, 13

limestone, 12

machinery, 5, 7–13, 16, 17, 20, 23, 27
magnetometer, 4
metals, 3, 8, 10, 11
mills. *See* concentrating mills and
    steel mills
minerals, 3, 5, 8, 20, 26
mines, 3, 4, 6, 7, 8, 9, 14, 15, 16,
    28, 29
molybdenum, 3, 5, 8, 13, 28
molds, 13

oil, 11, 15, 18, 19, 20–24, 30
oil pump, 19
oil refineries, 21, 22, 23
oil spills, 27
oil tanks, 21, 22, 23
oil well, 15, 19, 20
ore, 7–12, 27, 29
ore cages, 7, 9. *See also* elevators
overburden, 16, 28

pellets, 11, 12
petrochemical plants, 24
pipelines, 21, 23
plants. *See* wildlife
plastic, 2, 24
pollution, 26, 27,
pumping stations, 21

recycling, 29
refining, 11, 12, 21, 22, 23, 24, 27
remote control, 9
roughnecks, 20

samples, rock, 5
satellites, 4
shaft mines, 6–7
smelters, 11
steel, 2–3, 11, 12, 13, 20, 30
steel products, 13, 30
surface mines, 15–17

tailings, 12, 28, 29
temperature, 6, 21, 22
tunnels, 6, 29

ventilation, 6

waste, 10, 11, 12, 24, 28, 29
water, 15, 18, 20, 27
wellhead, 20
wildlife, 26, 27, 28, 29

This book is dedicated to my hockey players, Brian, Steph and Moo — J.D.

The authors gratefully acknowledge the assistance of Jack Van Alstine; Fred Brooks;
Jane Crist; Jim, Stephanie, Brian and Madeline Drake; Tom and Cindy Drake; Jackie Evanger; Hal Fitch;
Al Johnson; Bob Keyes; Peter McBride; Cy Morgan; John Morgan; Johnnie Morrison; Fred Newton;
Peter Newton; Deborah Nicely, Nordberg Inc. Global Mining Division; Liz Roca-Crooks, National Mining
Association; Tom Ryley; Mary and Doug Thompson; Mark Wolfe.

Thanks to Valerie Hussey, Ricky Englander and all the people at Kids Can Press. A special thank you to
Pat Cupples, Debbie Rogosin, Trudee Romanek, Marie Bartholomew, Laura Ellis and Lynda Prince.

First U.S. edition 1999

Text copyright © 1997 by Jane Drake and Ann Love
Illustrations copyright © 1997 by Pat Cupples

The artwork in this book was rendered in watercolor, gouache,
graphite and colored pencil on hot-press watercolor paper.

Published in Canada by
Kids Can Press Ltd.
29 Birch Avenue
Toronto, ON M4V 1E2

Published in the U.S. by
Kids Can Press Ltd.
85 River Rock Drive, Suite 202
Buffalo, NY 14207

Edited by Debbie Rogosin and Trudee Romanek
Designed by Marie Bartholomew and Karen Powers
Printed in Hong Kong by Sheck Wah Tong Printing Press Limited

US 99 0 9 8 7 6 5 4 3 2 1

Canadian Cataloguing in Publication Data

Drake, Jane
    Mining

(America at work)
Includes index.
ISBN 1-55074-508-5

1. Mining engineering — United States — Juvenile literature.
2. Mines and mineral resources — United States — Juvenile
literature. I. Love, Ann. II. Cupples, Patricia. III. Title.
IV. Series: America at work (Toronto, Ont.).

TN148.D72 1999   j622'.0973   C99-930581-6

Kids Can Press is a Nelvana company